AF867397

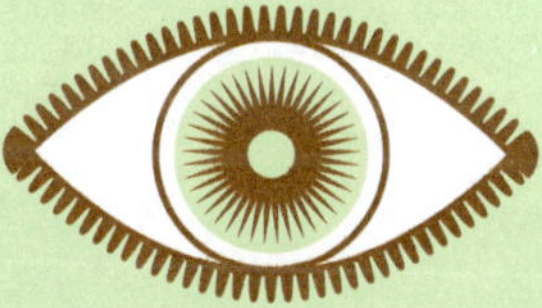

A Sweet Hearts Press book
An imprint of Moore Street Media
50/99 Moore Street
Leichhardt NSW 2040
Australia

sweetheartspress.com
Follow us! sweethearts_press
Tag #sweetheartspress to show us your pics

ISBN: 9781922468642

Published in 2026 by Sweet Hearts Press
Copyright text and design © Moore Street Media 2026

All rights reserved. No part of this publication may be reproduced, stored in a retrieval system, or transmitted in any form or by any means, electronic, mechanical, photocopying, recording or otherwise, without the prior written permission of the publisher.

Note: This book may not be used, in whole or in part, for the training of artificial intelligence (AI) systems.

Designed by Sweet Hearts Press

Printed and bound in China
10 9 8 7 6 5 4 3 2 1

DEFINITELY NOT MY

INTERNET PASSWORDS

A PLACE TO KEEP ALL YOUR PASSCODES, LOG-INS, AND PASSWORDS OFFLINE

Sweet Hearts Press

A POCKET-SIZED VAULT
FOR YOUR DIGITAL WORLD!

THIS NOTEBOOK OFFERS
A DISCREET OFFLINE WAY
TO STORE YOUR MOST
IMPORTANT PASSCODES,
LOG-INS, AND OTHER
PRIVATE DETAILS.
SIMPLY REMOVE THE TITLE
STICKER ON THE COVER
FOR ANONYMITY.

APPLICATION/WEB ADDRESS

USERNAME

PASSWORD

PASSWORD HINTS

APPLICATION/WEB ADDRESS

USERNAME

PASSWORD

PASSWORD HINTS

APPLICATION/WEB ADDRESS

USERNAME

PASSWORD

PASSWORD HINTS

APPLICATION/WEB ADDRESS

USERNAME

PASSWORD

PASSWORD HINTS

APPLICATION/WEB ADDRESS

USERNAME

PASSWORD

PASSWORD HINTS

APPLICATION/WEB ADDRESS

USERNAME

PASSWORD

PASSWORD HINTS

APPLICATION/WEB ADDRESS

USERNAME

PASSWORD

PASSWORD HINTS

APPLICATION/WEB ADDRESS

USERNAME

PASSWORD

PASSWORD HINTS

APPLICATION/WEB ADDRESS

USERNAME

PASSWORD

PASSWORD HINTS

APPLICATION/WEB ADDRESS

USERNAME

PASSWORD

PASSWORD HINTS

APPLICATION/WEB ADDRESS

USERNAME

PASSWORD

PASSWORD HINTS

APPLICATION/WEB ADDRESS

USERNAME

PASSWORD

PASSWORD HINTS

APPLICATION/WEB ADDRESS

USERNAME

PASSWORD

PASSWORD HINTS

APPLICATION/WEB ADDRESS

USERNAME

PASSWORD

PASSWORD HINTS

APPLICATION/WEB ADDRESS

USERNAME

PASSWORD

PASSWORD HINTS

APPLICATION/WEB ADDRESS

USERNAME

PASSWORD

PASSWORD HINTS

APPLICATION/WEB ADDRESS

USERNAME

PASSWORD

PASSWORD HINTS

APPLICATION/WEB ADDRESS

USERNAME

PASSWORD

PASSWORD HINTS

APPLICATION/WEB ADDRESS

USERNAME

PASSWORD

PASSWORD HINTS

APPLICATION/WEB ADDRESS

USERNAME

PASSWORD

PASSWORD HINTS

APPLICATION/WEB ADDRESS

USERNAME

PASSWORD

PASSWORD HINTS

APPLICATION/WEB ADDRESS

USERNAME

PASSWORD

PASSWORD HINTS

APPLICATION/WEB ADDRESS

USERNAME

PASSWORD

PASSWORD HINTS

APPLICATION/WEB ADDRESS

USERNAME

PASSWORD

PASSWORD HINTS

APPLICATION/WEB ADDRESS

USERNAME

PASSWORD

PASSWORD HINTS

APPLICATION/WEB ADDRESS

USERNAME

PASSWORD

PASSWORD HINTS

B

APPLICATION/WEB ADDRESS

USERNAME

PASSWORD

PASSWORD HINTS

APPLICATION/WEB ADDRESS

USERNAME

PASSWORD

PASSWORD HINTS

APPLICATION/WEB ADDRESS

USERNAME

PASSWORD

PASSWORD HINTS

APPLICATION/WEB ADDRESS

USERNAME

PASSWORD

PASSWORD HINTS

APPLICATION/WEB ADDRESS

USERNAME

PASSWORD

PASSWORD HINTS

APPLICATION/WEB ADDRESS

USERNAME

PASSWORD

PASSWORD HINTS

APPLICATION/WEB ADDRESS

USERNAME

PASSWORD

PASSWORD HINTS

APPLICATION/WEB ADDRESS

USERNAME

PASSWORD

PASSWORD HINTS

APPLICATION/WEB ADDRESS

USERNAME

PASSWORD

PASSWORD HINTS

APPLICATION/WEB ADDRESS

USERNAME

PASSWORD

PASSWORD HINTS

APPLICATION/WEB ADDRESS

USERNAME

PASSWORD

PASSWORD HINTS

APPLICATION/WEB ADDRESS

USERNAME

PASSWORD

PASSWORD HINTS

APPLICATION/WEB ADDRESS

USERNAME

PASSWORD

PASSWORD HINTS

APPLICATION/WEB ADDRESS

USERNAME

PASSWORD

PASSWORD HINTS

APPLICATION/WEB ADDRESS

USERNAME

PASSWORD

PASSWORD HINTS

APPLICATION/WEB ADDRESS

USERNAME

PASSWORD

PASSWORD HINTS

APPLICATION/WEB ADDRESS

USERNAME

PASSWORD

PASSWORD HINTS

APPLICATION/WEB ADDRESS

USERNAME

PASSWORD

PASSWORD HINTS

APPLICATION/WEB ADDRESS

USERNAME

PASSWORD

PASSWORD HINTS

APPLICATION/WEB ADDRESS

USERNAME

PASSWORD

PASSWORD HINTS

APPLICATION/WEB ADDRESS

USERNAME

PASSWORD

PASSWORD HINTS

APPLICATION/WEB ADDRESS

USERNAME

PASSWORD

PASSWORD HINTS

D

APPLICATION/WEB ADDRESS

USERNAME

PASSWORD

PASSWORD HINTS

APPLICATION/WEB ADDRESS

USERNAME

PASSWORD

PASSWORD HINTS

D

APPLICATION/WEB ADDRESS

USERNAME

PASSWORD

PASSWORD HINTS

APPLICATION/WEB ADDRESS

USERNAME

PASSWORD

PASSWORD HINTS

D

APPLICATION/WEB ADDRESS

USERNAME

PASSWORD

PASSWORD HINTS

APPLICATION/WEB ADDRESS

USERNAME

PASSWORD

PASSWORD HINTS

D

APPLICATION/WEB ADDRESS

USERNAME

PASSWORD

PASSWORD HINTS

APPLICATION/WEB ADDRESS

USERNAME

PASSWORD

PASSWORD HINTS

APPLICATION/WEB ADDRESS

USERNAME

PASSWORD

PASSWORD HINTS

D

APPLICATION/WEB ADDRESS

USERNAME

PASSWORD

PASSWORD HINTS

D

APPLICATION/WEB ADDRESS

USERNAME

PASSWORD

PASSWORD HINTS

APPLICATION/WEB ADDRESS

USERNAME

PASSWORD

PASSWORD HINTS

D

APPLICATION/WEB ADDRESS

USERNAME

PASSWORD

PASSWORD HINTS

APPLICATION/WEB ADDRESS

USERNAME

PASSWORD

PASSWORD HINTS

D

APPLICATION/WEB ADDRESS

USERNAME

PASSWORD

PASSWORD HINTS

APPLICATION/WEB ADDRESS

USERNAME

PASSWORD

PASSWORD HINTS

APPLICATION/WEB ADDRESS

USERNAME

PASSWORD

PASSWORD HINTS

APPLICATION/WEB ADDRESS

USERNAME

PASSWORD

PASSWORD HINTS

APPLICATION/WEB ADDRESS

USERNAME

PASSWORD

PASSWORD HINTS

APPLICATION/WEB ADDRESS

USERNAME

PASSWORD

PASSWORD HINTS

APPLICATION/WEB ADDRESS

USERNAME

PASSWORD

PASSWORD HINTS

APPLICATION/WEB ADDRESS

USERNAME

PASSWORD

PASSWORD HINTS

APPLICATION/WEB ADDRESS

USERNAME

PASSWORD

PASSWORD HINTS

APPLICATION/WEB ADDRESS

USERNAME

PASSWORD

PASSWORD HINTS

APPLICATION/WEB ADDRESS

USERNAME

PASSWORD

PASSWORD HINTS

APPLICATION/WEB ADDRESS

USERNAME

PASSWORD

PASSWORD HINTS

APPLICATION/WEB ADDRESS

USERNAME

PASSWORD

PASSWORD HINTS

APPLICATION/WEB ADDRESS

USERNAME

PASSWORD

PASSWORD HINTS

APPLICATION/WEB ADDRESS

USERNAME

PASSWORD

PASSWORD HINTS

APPLICATION/WEB ADDRESS

USERNAME

PASSWORD

PASSWORD HINTS

APPLICATION/WEB ADDRESS

USERNAME

PASSWORD

PASSWORD HINTS

APPLICATION/WEB ADDRESS

USERNAME

PASSWORD

PASSWORD HINTS

APPLICATION/WEB ADDRESS

USERNAME

PASSWORD

PASSWORD HINTS

APPLICATION/WEB ADDRESS

USERNAME

PASSWORD

PASSWORD HINTS

F

F

APPLICATION/WEB ADDRESS

USERNAME

PASSWORD

PASSWORD HINTS

APPLICATION/WEB ADDRESS

USERNAME

PASSWORD

PASSWORD HINTS

APPLICATION/WEB ADDRESS

USERNAME

PASSWORD

PASSWORD HINTS

APPLICATION/WEB ADDRESS

USERNAME

PASSWORD

PASSWORD HINTS

F

APPLICATION/WEB ADDRESS

USERNAME

PASSWORD

PASSWORD HINTS

APPLICATION/WEB ADDRESS

USERNAME

PASSWORD

PASSWORD HINTS

F

APPLICATION/WEB ADDRESS

USERNAME

PASSWORD

PASSWORD HINTS

APPLICATION/WEB ADDRESS

USERNAME

PASSWORD

PASSWORD HINTS

F

APPLICATION/WEB ADDRESS

USERNAME

PASSWORD

PASSWORD HINTS

APPLICATION/WEB ADDRESS

USERNAME

PASSWORD

PASSWORD HINTS

APPLICATION/WEB ADDRESS

USERNAME

PASSWORD

PASSWORD HINTS

APPLICATION/WEB ADDRESS

USERNAME

PASSWORD

PASSWORD HINTS

F

F

APPLICATION/WEB ADDRESS

USERNAME

PASSWORD

PASSWORD HINTS

APPLICATION/WEB ADDRESS

USERNAME

PASSWORD

PASSWORD HINTS

APPLICATION/WEB ADDRESS

USERNAME

PASSWORD

PASSWORD HINTS

APPLICATION/WEB ADDRESS

USERNAME

PASSWORD

PASSWORD HINTS

APPLICATION/WEB ADDRESS

USERNAME

PASSWORD

PASSWORD HINTS

APPLICATION/WEB ADDRESS

USERNAME

PASSWORD

PASSWORD HINTS

APPLICATION/WEB ADDRESS

USERNAME

PASSWORD

PASSWORD HINTS

APPLICATION/WEB ADDRESS

USERNAME

PASSWORD

PASSWORD HINTS

APPLICATION/WEB ADDRESS

USERNAME

PASSWORD

PASSWORD HINTS

APPLICATION/WEB ADDRESS

USERNAME

PASSWORD

PASSWORD HINTS

APPLICATION/WEB ADDRESS

USERNAME

PASSWORD

PASSWORD HINTS

APPLICATION/WEB ADDRESS

USERNAME

PASSWORD

PASSWORD HINTS

APPLICATION/WEB ADDRESS

USERNAME

PASSWORD

PASSWORD HINTS

APPLICATION/WEB ADDRESS

USERNAME

PASSWORD

PASSWORD HINTS

APPLICATION/WEB ADDRESS

USERNAME

PASSWORD

PASSWORD HINTS

APPLICATION/WEB ADDRESS

USERNAME

PASSWORD

PASSWORD HINTS

APPLICATION/WEB ADDRESS

USERNAME

PASSWORD

PASSWORD HINTS

APPLICATION/WEB ADDRESS

USERNAME

PASSWORD

PASSWORD HINTS

APPLICATION/WEB ADDRESS

USERNAME

PASSWORD

PASSWORD HINTS

APPLICATION/WEB ADDRESS

USERNAME

PASSWORD

PASSWORD HINTS

APPLICATION/WEB ADDRESS

USERNAME

PASSWORD

PASSWORD HINTS

APPLICATION/WEB ADDRESS

USERNAME

PASSWORD

PASSWORD HINTS

APPLICATION/WEB ADDRESS

USERNAME

PASSWORD

PASSWORD HINTS

APPLICATION/WEB ADDRESS

USERNAME

PASSWORD

PASSWORD HINTS

H

APPLICATION/WEB ADDRESS

USERNAME

PASSWORD

PASSWORD HINTS

APPLICATION/WEB ADDRESS

USERNAME

PASSWORD

PASSWORD HINTS

APPLICATION/WEB ADDRESS

USERNAME

PASSWORD

PASSWORD HINTS

APPLICATION/WEB ADDRESS

USERNAME

PASSWORD

PASSWORD HINTS

H

H

APPLICATION/WEB ADDRESS

USERNAME

PASSWORD

PASSWORD HINTS

APPLICATION/WEB ADDRESS

USERNAME

PASSWORD

PASSWORD HINTS

APPLICATION/WEB ADDRESS

USERNAME

PASSWORD

PASSWORD HINTS

APPLICATION/WEB ADDRESS

USERNAME

PASSWORD

PASSWORD HINTS

H

APPLICATION/WEB ADDRESS

USERNAME

PASSWORD

PASSWORD HINTS

APPLICATION/WEB ADDRESS

USERNAME

PASSWORD

PASSWORD HINTS

APPLICATION/WEB ADDRESS

USERNAME

PASSWORD

PASSWORD HINTS

APPLICATION/WEB ADDRESS

USERNAME

PASSWORD

PASSWORD HINTS

APPLICATION/WEB ADDRESS

USERNAME

PASSWORD

PASSWORD HINTS

APPLICATION/WEB ADDRESS

USERNAME

PASSWORD

PASSWORD HINTS

APPLICATION/WEB ADDRESS

USERNAME

PASSWORD

PASSWORD HINTS

APPLICATION/WEB ADDRESS

USERNAME

PASSWORD

PASSWORD HINTS

APPLICATION/WEB ADDRESS

USERNAME

PASSWORD

PASSWORD HINTS

APPLICATION/WEB ADDRESS

USERNAME

PASSWORD

PASSWORD HINTS

APPLICATION/WEB ADDRESS

USERNAME

PASSWORD

PASSWORD HINTS

APPLICATION/WEB ADDRESS

USERNAME

PASSWORD

PASSWORD HINTS

APPLICATION/WEB ADDRESS

USERNAME

PASSWORD

PASSWORD HINTS

APPLICATION/WEB ADDRESS

USERNAME

PASSWORD

PASSWORD HINTS

APPLICATION/WEB ADDRESS

USERNAME

PASSWORD

PASSWORD HINTS

APPLICATION/WEB ADDRESS

USERNAME

PASSWORD

PASSWORD HINTS

APPLICATION/WEB ADDRESS

USERNAME

PASSWORD

PASSWORD HINTS

APPLICATION/WEB ADDRESS

USERNAME

PASSWORD

PASSWORD HINTS

APPLICATION/WEB ADDRESS

USERNAME

PASSWORD

PASSWORD HINTS

J

APPLICATION/WEB ADDRESS

USERNAME

PASSWORD

PASSWORD HINTS

APPLICATION/WEB ADDRESS

USERNAME

PASSWORD

J

PASSWORD HINTS

APPLICATION/WEB ADDRESS

USERNAME

PASSWORD

PASSWORD HINTS

APPLICATION/WEB ADDRESS

USERNAME

PASSWORD

PASSWORD HINTS

APPLICATION/WEB ADDRESS

USERNAME

PASSWORD

PASSWORD HINTS

APPLICATION/WEB ADDRESS

USERNAME

PASSWORD

J

PASSWORD HINTS

APPLICATION/WEB ADDRESS

USERNAME

PASSWORD

PASSWORD HINTS

APPLICATION/WEB ADDRESS

USERNAME

PASSWORD

PASSWORD HINTS

J

APPLICATION/WEB ADDRESS

USERNAME

PASSWORD

PASSWORD HINTS

APPLICATION/WEB ADDRESS

USERNAME

PASSWORD

J

PASSWORD HINTS

APPLICATION/WEB ADDRESS

USERNAME

PASSWORD

PASSWORD HINTS

APPLICATION/WEB ADDRESS

USERNAME

PASSWORD

PASSWORD HINTS

J

APPLICATION/WEB ADDRESS

USERNAME

PASSWORD

PASSWORD HINTS

J

APPLICATION/WEB ADDRESS

USERNAME

PASSWORD

PASSWORD HINTS

APPLICATION/WEB ADDRESS

USERNAME

PASSWORD

PASSWORD HINTS

APPLICATION/WEB ADDRESS

USERNAME

PASSWORD

PASSWORD HINTS

APPLICATION/WEB ADDRESS

USERNAME

PASSWORD

PASSWORD HINTS

APPLICATION/WEB ADDRESS

USERNAME

PASSWORD

PASSWORD HINTS

APPLICATION/WEB ADDRESS

USERNAME

PASSWORD

PASSWORD HINTS

APPLICATION/WEB ADDRESS

USERNAME

PASSWORD

PASSWORD HINTS

APPLICATION/WEB ADDRESS

USERNAME

PASSWORD

PASSWORD HINTS

APPLICATION/WEB ADDRESS

USERNAME

PASSWORD

PASSWORD HINTS

APPLICATION/WEB ADDRESS

USERNAME

PASSWORD

PASSWORD HINTS

APPLICATION/WEB ADDRESS

USERNAME

PASSWORD

PASSWORD HINTS

APPLICATION/WEB ADDRESS

USERNAME

PASSWORD

PASSWORD HINTS

APPLICATION/WEB ADDRESS

USERNAME

PASSWORD

PASSWORD HINTS

APPLICATION/WEB ADDRESS

USERNAME

PASSWORD

PASSWORD HINTS

APPLICATION/WEB ADDRESS

USERNAME

PASSWORD

PASSWORD HINTS

APPLICATION/WEB ADDRESS

USERNAME

PASSWORD

PASSWORD HINTS

APPLICATION/WEB ADDRESS

USERNAME

PASSWORD

PASSWORD HINTS

APPLICATION/WEB ADDRESS

USERNAME

PASSWORD

PASSWORD HINTS

APPLICATION/WEB ADDRESS

USERNAME

PASSWORD

PASSWORD HINTS

L

APPLICATION/WEB ADDRESS

USERNAME

PASSWORD

PASSWORD HINTS

APPLICATION/WEB ADDRESS

USERNAME

PASSWORD

PASSWORD HINTS

L

APPLICATION/WEB ADDRESS

USERNAME

PASSWORD

PASSWORD HINTS

APPLICATION/WEB ADDRESS

USERNAME

PASSWORD

PASSWORD HINTS

L

APPLICATION/WEB ADDRESS

USERNAME

PASSWORD

PASSWORD HINTS

APPLICATION/WEB ADDRESS

USERNAME

PASSWORD

PASSWORD HINTS

L

APPLICATION/WEB ADDRESS

USERNAME

PASSWORD

PASSWORD HINTS

APPLICATION/WEB ADDRESS

USERNAME

PASSWORD

PASSWORD HINTS

L

APPLICATION/WEB ADDRESS

USERNAME

PASSWORD

PASSWORD HINTS

APPLICATION/WEB ADDRESS

USERNAME

PASSWORD

PASSWORD HINTS

L

APPLICATION/WEB ADDRESS

USERNAME

PASSWORD

PASSWORD HINTS

APPLICATION/WEB ADDRESS

USERNAME

PASSWORD

PASSWORD HINTS

L

APPLICATION/WEB ADDRESS

USERNAME

PASSWORD

PASSWORD HINTS

APPLICATION/WEB ADDRESS

USERNAME

PASSWORD

PASSWORD HINTS

L

APPLICATION/WEB ADDRESS

USERNAME

PASSWORD

PASSWORD HINTS

APPLICATION/WEB ADDRESS

USERNAME

PASSWORD

PASSWORD HINTS

APPLICATION/WEB ADDRESS

USERNAME

PASSWORD

PASSWORD HINTS

APPLICATION/WEB ADDRESS

USERNAME

PASSWORD

PASSWORD HINTS

APPLICATION/WEB ADDRESS

USERNAME

PASSWORD

PASSWORD HINTS

APPLICATION/WEB ADDRESS

USERNAME

PASSWORD

PASSWORD HINTS

APPLICATION/WEB ADDRESS

USERNAME

PASSWORD

PASSWORD HINTS

APPLICATION/WEB ADDRESS

USERNAME

PASSWORD

PASSWORD HINTS

APPLICATION/WEB ADDRESS

USERNAME

PASSWORD

PASSWORD HINTS

APPLICATION/WEB ADDRESS

USERNAME

PASSWORD

PASSWORD HINTS

APPLICATION/WEB ADDRESS

USERNAME

PASSWORD

PASSWORD HINTS

APPLICATION/WEB ADDRESS

USERNAME

PASSWORD

PASSWORD HINTS

APPLICATION/WEB ADDRESS

USERNAME

PASSWORD

PASSWORD HINTS

APPLICATION/WEB ADDRESS

USERNAME

PASSWORD

PASSWORD HINTS

APPLICATION/WEB ADDRESS

USERNAME

PASSWORD

PASSWORD HINTS

APPLICATION/WEB ADDRESS

USERNAME

PASSWORD

PASSWORD HINTS

APPLICATION/WEB ADDRESS

USERNAME

PASSWORD

PASSWORD HINTS

APPLICATION/WEB ADDRESS

USERNAME

PASSWORD

PASSWORD HINTS

APPLICATION/WEB ADDRESS

USERNAME

PASSWORD

PASSWORD HINTS

APPLICATION/WEB ADDRESS

USERNAME

PASSWORD

PASSWORD HINTS

N

APPLICATION/WEB ADDRESS

USERNAME

PASSWORD

PASSWORD HINTS

APPLICATION/WEB ADDRESS

USERNAME

PASSWORD

PASSWORD HINTS

N

APPLICATION/WEB ADDRESS

USERNAME

PASSWORD

PASSWORD HINTS

APPLICATION/WEB ADDRESS

USERNAME

PASSWORD

PASSWORD HINTS

N

APPLICATION/WEB ADDRESS

USERNAME

PASSWORD

PASSWORD HINTS

APPLICATION/WEB ADDRESS

USERNAME

PASSWORD

PASSWORD HINTS

N

APPLICATION/WEB ADDRESS

USERNAME

PASSWORD

PASSWORD HINTS

APPLICATION/WEB ADDRESS

USERNAME

PASSWORD

PASSWORD HINTS

N

APPLICATION/WEB ADDRESS

USERNAME

PASSWORD

PASSWORD HINTS

APPLICATION/WEB ADDRESS

USERNAME

PASSWORD

PASSWORD HINTS

N

APPLICATION/WEB ADDRESS

USERNAME

PASSWORD

PASSWORD HINTS

APPLICATION/WEB ADDRESS

USERNAME

PASSWORD

PASSWORD HINTS

APPLICATION/WEB ADDRESS

USERNAME

PASSWORD

PASSWORD HINTS

APPLICATION/WEB ADDRESS

USERNAME

PASSWORD

PASSWORD HINTS

APPLICATION/WEB ADDRESS

USERNAME

PASSWORD

PASSWORD HINTS

APPLICATION/WEB ADDRESS

USERNAME

PASSWORD

PASSWORD HINTS

APPLICATION/WEB ADDRESS

USERNAME

PASSWORD

PASSWORD HINTS

APPLICATION/WEB ADDRESS

USERNAME

PASSWORD

PASSWORD HINTS

APPLICATION/WEB ADDRESS

USERNAME

PASSWORD

PASSWORD HINTS

APPLICATION/WEB ADDRESS

USERNAME

PASSWORD

PASSWORD HINTS

APPLICATION/WEB ADDRESS

USERNAME

PASSWORD

PASSWORD HINTS

APPLICATION/WEB ADDRESS

USERNAME

PASSWORD

PASSWORD HINTS

APPLICATION/WEB ADDRESS

USERNAME

PASSWORD

PASSWORD HINTS

APPLICATION/WEB ADDRESS

USERNAME

PASSWORD

PASSWORD HINTS

APPLICATION/WEB ADDRESS

USERNAME

PASSWORD

PASSWORD HINTS

APPLICATION/WEB ADDRESS

USERNAME

PASSWORD

PASSWORD HINTS

APPLICATION/WEB ADDRESS

USERNAME

PASSWORD

PASSWORD HINTS

APPLICATION/WEB ADDRESS

USERNAME

PASSWORD

PASSWORD HINTS

APPLICATION/WEB ADDRESS

USERNAME

PASSWORD

PASSWORD HINTS

APPLICATION/WEB ADDRESS

USERNAME

PASSWORD

PASSWORD HINTS

APPLICATION/WEB ADDRESS

USERNAME

PASSWORD

PASSWORD HINTS

APPLICATION/WEB ADDRESS

USERNAME

PASSWORD

PASSWORD HINTS

APPLICATION/WEB ADDRESS

USERNAME

PASSWORD

PASSWORD HINTS

APPLICATION/WEB ADDRESS

USERNAME

PASSWORD

PASSWORD HINTS

APPLICATION/WEB ADDRESS

USERNAME

PASSWORD

PASSWORD HINTS

APPLICATION/WEB ADDRESS

USERNAME

PASSWORD

PASSWORD HINTS

APPLICATION/WEB ADDRESS

USERNAME

PASSWORD

PASSWORD HINTS

P

APPLICATION/WEB ADDRESS

USERNAME

PASSWORD

PASSWORD HINTS

APPLICATION/WEB ADDRESS

USERNAME

PASSWORD

PASSWORD HINTS

P

APPLICATION/WEB ADDRESS

USERNAME

PASSWORD

PASSWORD HINTS

APPLICATION/WEB ADDRESS

USERNAME

PASSWORD

PASSWORD HINTS

APPLICATION/WEB ADDRESS

USERNAME

PASSWORD

PASSWORD HINTS

APPLICATION/WEB ADDRESS

USERNAME

PASSWORD

PASSWORD HINTS

APPLICATION/WEB ADDRESS

USERNAME

PASSWORD

PASSWORD HINTS

APPLICATION/WEB ADDRESS

P

USERNAME

PASSWORD

PASSWORD HINTS

APPLICATION/WEB ADDRESS

USERNAME

PASSWORD

PASSWORD HINTS

APPLICATION/WEB ADDRESS

USERNAME

PASSWORD

PASSWORD HINTS

APPLICATION/WEB ADDRESS

USERNAME

PASSWORD

PASSWORD HINTS

APPLICATION/WEB ADDRESS

USERNAME

PASSWORD

PASSWORD HINTS

APPLICATION/WEB ADDRESS

USERNAME

PASSWORD

PASSWORD HINTS

APPLICATION/WEB ADDRESS

USERNAME

PASSWORD

PASSWORD HINTS

APPLICATION/WEB ADDRESS

USERNAME

PASSWORD

PASSWORD HINTS

APPLICATION/WEB ADDRESS

USERNAME

PASSWORD

PASSWORD HINTS

APPLICATION/WEB ADDRESS

USERNAME

PASSWORD

PASSWORD HINTS

APPLICATION/WEB ADDRESS

USERNAME

PASSWORD

PASSWORD HINTS

APPLICATION/WEB ADDRESS

USERNAME

PASSWORD

PASSWORD HINTS

APPLICATION/WEB ADDRESS

USERNAME

PASSWORD

PASSWORD HINTS

APPLICATION/WEB ADDRESS

USERNAME

PASSWORD

PASSWORD HINTS

APPLICATION/WEB ADDRESS

USERNAME

PASSWORD

PASSWORD HINTS

APPLICATION/WEB ADDRESS

USERNAME

PASSWORD

PASSWORD HINTS

APPLICATION/WEB ADDRESS

USERNAME

PASSWORD

PASSWORD HINTS

APPLICATION/WEB ADDRESS

USERNAME

PASSWORD

PASSWORD HINTS

APPLICATION/WEB ADDRESS

USERNAME

PASSWORD

PASSWORD HINTS

R

APPLICATION/WEB ADDRESS

USERNAME

PASSWORD

PASSWORD HINTS

APPLICATION/WEB ADDRESS

USERNAME

PASSWORD

PASSWORD HINTS

APPLICATION/WEB ADDRESS

USERNAME

PASSWORD

PASSWORD HINTS

APPLICATION/WEB ADDRESS

USERNAME

PASSWORD

PASSWORD HINTS

R

APPLICATION/WEB ADDRESS

USERNAME

PASSWORD

PASSWORD HINTS

APPLICATION/WEB ADDRESS

USERNAME

PASSWORD

PASSWORD HINTS

R

APPLICATION/WEB ADDRESS

USERNAME

PASSWORD

PASSWORD HINTS

APPLICATION/WEB ADDRESS

USERNAME

PASSWORD

PASSWORD HINTS

APPLICATION/WEB ADDRESS

USERNAME

PASSWORD

PASSWORD HINTS

APPLICATION/WEB ADDRESS

R

USERNAME

PASSWORD

PASSWORD HINTS

APPLICATION/WEB ADDRESS

USERNAME

PASSWORD

PASSWORD HINTS

APPLICATION/WEB ADDRESS

USERNAME

PASSWORD

PASSWORD HINTS

APPLICATION/WEB ADDRESS

USERNAME

PASSWORD

PASSWORD HINTS

APPLICATION/WEB ADDRESS

USERNAME

PASSWORD

PASSWORD HINTS

APPLICATION/WEB ADDRESS

USERNAME

PASSWORD

PASSWORD HINTS

APPLICATION/WEB ADDRESS

USERNAME

PASSWORD

PASSWORD HINTS

APPLICATION/WEB ADDRESS

USERNAME

PASSWORD

PASSWORD HINTS

APPLICATION/WEB ADDRESS

USERNAME

PASSWORD

PASSWORD HINTS

APPLICATION/WEB ADDRESS

USERNAME

PASSWORD

PASSWORD HINTS

APPLICATION/WEB ADDRESS

USERNAME

PASSWORD

PASSWORD HINTS

APPLICATION/WEB ADDRESS

USERNAME

PASSWORD

PASSWORD HINTS

APPLICATION/WEB ADDRESS

USERNAME

PASSWORD

PASSWORD HINTS

APPLICATION/WEB ADDRESS

USERNAME

PASSWORD

PASSWORD HINTS

APPLICATION/WEB ADDRESS

USERNAME

PASSWORD

PASSWORD HINTS

APPLICATION/WEB ADDRESS

USERNAME

PASSWORD

PASSWORD HINTS

APPLICATION/WEB ADDRESS

USERNAME

PASSWORD

PASSWORD HINTS

APPLICATION/WEB ADDRESS

USERNAME

PASSWORD

PASSWORD HINTS

APPLICATION/WEB ADDRESS

USERNAME

PASSWORD

PASSWORD HINTS

APPLICATION/WEB ADDRESS

USERNAME

PASSWORD

PASSWORD HINTS

APPLICATION/WEB ADDRESS

USERNAME

PASSWORD

PASSWORD HINTS

APPLICATION/WEB ADDRESS

USERNAME

PASSWORD

PASSWORD HINTS

APPLICATION/WEB ADDRESS

USERNAME

PASSWORD

PASSWORD HINTS

APPLICATION/WEB ADDRESS

USERNAME

PASSWORD

PASSWORD HINTS

APPLICATION/WEB ADDRESS

USERNAME

PASSWORD

PASSWORD HINTS

T

APPLICATION/WEB ADDRESS

USERNAME

PASSWORD

PASSWORD HINTS

APPLICATION/WEB ADDRESS

USERNAME

PASSWORD

PASSWORD HINTS

T

APPLICATION/WEB ADDRESS

USERNAME

PASSWORD

PASSWORD HINTS

APPLICATION/WEB ADDRESS

USERNAME

PASSWORD

PASSWORD HINTS

T

APPLICATION/WEB ADDRESS

USERNAME

PASSWORD

PASSWORD HINTS

APPLICATION/WEB ADDRESS

USERNAME

PASSWORD

PASSWORD HINTS

APPLICATION/WEB ADDRESS

USERNAME

PASSWORD

PASSWORD HINTS

APPLICATION/WEB ADDRESS

USERNAME

PASSWORD

PASSWORD HINTS

T

APPLICATION/WEB ADDRESS

USERNAME

PASSWORD

PASSWORD HINTS

APPLICATION/WEB ADDRESS

USERNAME

PASSWORD

PASSWORD HINTS

APPLICATION/WEB ADDRESS

USERNAME

PASSWORD

PASSWORD HINTS

APPLICATION/WEB ADDRESS

USERNAME

PASSWORD

PASSWORD HINTS

APPLICATION/WEB ADDRESS

USERNAME

PASSWORD

PASSWORD HINTS

APPLICATION/WEB ADDRESS

USERNAME

PASSWORD

PASSWORD HINTS

APPLICATION/WEB ADDRESS

USERNAME

PASSWORD

PASSWORD HINTS

APPLICATION/WEB ADDRESS

USERNAME

PASSWORD

PASSWORD HINTS

APPLICATION/WEB ADDRESS

USERNAME

PASSWORD

PASSWORD HINTS

APPLICATION/WEB ADDRESS

USERNAME

PASSWORD

PASSWORD HINTS

APPLICATION/WEB ADDRESS

USERNAME

PASSWORD

PASSWORD HINTS

APPLICATION/WEB ADDRESS

USERNAME

PASSWORD

PASSWORD HINTS

APPLICATION/WEB ADDRESS

USERNAME

PASSWORD

PASSWORD HINTS

APPLICATION/WEB ADDRESS

USERNAME

PASSWORD

PASSWORD HINTS

APPLICATION/WEB ADDRESS

USERNAME

PASSWORD

PASSWORD HINTS

APPLICATION/WEB ADDRESS

USERNAME

PASSWORD

PASSWORD HINTS

APPLICATION/WEB ADDRESS

USERNAME

PASSWORD

PASSWORD HINTS

APPLICATION/WEB ADDRESS

USERNAME

PASSWORD

PASSWORD HINTS

APPLICATION/WEB ADDRESS

USERNAME

PASSWORD

PASSWORD HINTS

APPLICATION/WEB ADDRESS

USERNAME

PASSWORD

PASSWORD HINTS

APPLICATION/WEB ADDRESS

USERNAME

PASSWORD

PASSWORD HINTS

APPLICATION/WEB ADDRESS

USERNAME

PASSWORD

PASSWORD HINTS

APPLICATION/WEB ADDRESS

USERNAME

PASSWORD

PASSWORD HINTS

APPLICATION/WEB ADDRESS

USERNAME

PASSWORD

PASSWORD HINTS

V

APPLICATION/WEB ADDRESS

USERNAME

PASSWORD

PASSWORD HINTS

APPLICATION/WEB ADDRESS

USERNAME

PASSWORD

PASSWORD HINTS

V

APPLICATION/WEB ADDRESS

USERNAME

PASSWORD

PASSWORD HINTS

APPLICATION/WEB ADDRESS

USERNAME

PASSWORD

PASSWORD HINTS

V

APPLICATION/WEB ADDRESS

USERNAME

PASSWORD

PASSWORD HINTS

APPLICATION/WEB ADDRESS

USERNAME

PASSWORD

PASSWORD HINTS

V

APPLICATION/WEB ADDRESS

USERNAME

PASSWORD

PASSWORD HINTS

APPLICATION/WEB ADDRESS

USERNAME

PASSWORD

PASSWORD HINTS

V

APPLICATION/WEB ADDRESS

USERNAME

PASSWORD

PASSWORD HINTS

APPLICATION/WEB ADDRESS

USERNAME

PASSWORD

PASSWORD HINTS

APPLICATION/WEB ADDRESS

USERNAME

PASSWORD

PASSWORD HINTS

APPLICATION/WEB ADDRESS

USERNAME

PASSWORD

V

PASSWORD HINTS

APPLICATION/WEB ADDRESS

USERNAME

PASSWORD

PASSWORD HINTS

APPLICATION/WEB ADDRESS

USERNAME

PASSWORD

PASSWORD HINTS

APPLICATION/WEB ADDRESS

USERNAME

PASSWORD

PASSWORD HINTS

APPLICATION/WEB ADDRESS

USERNAME

PASSWORD

PASSWORD HINTS

APPLICATION/WEB ADDRESS

USERNAME

PASSWORD

PASSWORD HINTS

APPLICATION/WEB ADDRESS

USERNAME

PASSWORD

PASSWORD HINTS

APPLICATION/WEB ADDRESS

USERNAME

PASSWORD

PASSWORD HINTS

APPLICATION/WEB ADDRESS

USERNAME

PASSWORD

PASSWORD HINTS

APPLICATION/WEB ADDRESS

USERNAME

PASSWORD

PASSWORD HINTS

APPLICATION/WEB ADDRESS

USERNAME

PASSWORD

PASSWORD HINTS

APPLICATION/WEB ADDRESS

USERNAME

PASSWORD

PASSWORD HINTS

APPLICATION/WEB ADDRESS

USERNAME

PASSWORD

PASSWORD HINTS

APPLICATION/WEB ADDRESS

USERNAME

PASSWORD

PASSWORD HINTS

APPLICATION/WEB ADDRESS

USERNAME

PASSWORD

PASSWORD HINTS

APPLICATION/WEB ADDRESS

USERNAME

PASSWORD

PASSWORD HINTS

APPLICATION/WEB ADDRESS

USERNAME

PASSWORD

PASSWORD HINTS

APPLICATION/WEB ADDRESS

USERNAME

PASSWORD

PASSWORD HINTS

APPLICATION/WEB ADDRESS

USERNAME

PASSWORD

PASSWORD HINTS

X

APPLICATION/WEB ADDRESS

USERNAME

PASSWORD

PASSWORD HINTS

APPLICATION/WEB ADDRESS

USERNAME

PASSWORD

PASSWORD HINTS

X

APPLICATION/WEB ADDRESS

USERNAME

PASSWORD

PASSWORD HINTS

APPLICATION/WEB ADDRESS

USERNAME

PASSWORD

PASSWORD HINTS

X

APPLICATION/WEB ADDRESS

USERNAME

PASSWORD

PASSWORD HINTS

APPLICATION/WEB ADDRESS

USERNAME

PASSWORD

PASSWORD HINTS

APPLICATION/WEB ADDRESS

USERNAME

PASSWORD

PASSWORD HINTS

APPLICATION/WEB ADDRESS

USERNAME

PASSWORD

PASSWORD HINTS

X

APPLICATION/WEB ADDRESS

USERNAME

PASSWORD

PASSWORD HINTS

APPLICATION/WEB ADDRESS

USERNAME

PASSWORD

PASSWORD HINTS

APPLICATION/WEB ADDRESS

USERNAME

PASSWORD

PASSWORD HINTS

APPLICATION/WEB ADDRESS

USERNAME

PASSWORD

PASSWORD HINTS

APPLICATION/WEB ADDRESS

USERNAME

PASSWORD

PASSWORD HINTS

APPLICATION/WEB ADDRESS

USERNAME

PASSWORD

PASSWORD HINTS

APPLICATION/WEB ADDRESS

USERNAME

PASSWORD

PASSWORD HINTS

APPLICATION/WEB ADDRESS

USERNAME

PASSWORD

PASSWORD HINTS

APPLICATION/WEB ADDRESS

USERNAME

PASSWORD

PASSWORD HINTS

APPLICATION/WEB ADDRESS

USERNAME

PASSWORD

PASSWORD HINTS

APPLICATION/WEB ADDRESS

USERNAME

PASSWORD

PASSWORD HINTS

APPLICATION/WEB ADDRESS

USERNAME

PASSWORD

PASSWORD HINTS

APPLICATION/WEB ADDRESS

USERNAME

PASSWORD

PASSWORD HINTS

APPLICATION/WEB ADDRESS

USERNAME

PASSWORD

PASSWORD HINTS

APPLICATION/WEB ADDRESS

USERNAME

PASSWORD

PASSWORD HINTS

APPLICATION/WEB ADDRESS

USERNAME

PASSWORD

PASSWORD HINTS

APPLICATION/WEB ADDRESS

USERNAME

PASSWORD

PASSWORD HINTS

APPLICATION/WEB ADDRESS

USERNAME

PASSWORD

PASSWORD HINTS

APPLICATION/WEB ADDRESS

USERNAME

PASSWORD

PASSWORD HINTS

APPLICATION/WEB ADDRESS

USERNAME

PASSWORD

PASSWORD HINTS

APPLICATION/WEB ADDRESS

USERNAME

PASSWORD

PASSWORD HINTS

APPLICATION/WEB ADDRESS

USERNAME

PASSWORD

PASSWORD HINTS

APPLICATION/WEB ADDRESS

USERNAME

PASSWORD

PASSWORD HINTS

APPLICATION/WEB ADDRESS

USERNAME

PASSWORD

PASSWORD HINTS

Z

APPLICATION/WEB ADDRESS

USERNAME

PASSWORD

PASSWORD HINTS

APPLICATION/WEB ADDRESS

USERNAME

PASSWORD

PASSWORD HINTS

APPLICATION/WEB ADDRESS

USERNAME

PASSWORD

PASSWORD HINTS

APPLICATION/WEB ADDRESS

USERNAME

PASSWORD

PASSWORD HINTS

APPLICATION/WEB ADDRESS

USERNAME

PASSWORD

PASSWORD HINTS

APPLICATION/WEB ADDRESS

USERNAME

PASSWORD

PASSWORD HINTS

APPLICATION/WEB ADDRESS

USERNAME

PASSWORD

PASSWORD HINTS

APPLICATION/WEB ADDRESS

USERNAME

PASSWORD

PASSWORD HINTS

APPLICATION/WEB ADDRESS

USERNAME

PASSWORD

PASSWORD HINTS

APPLICATION/WEB ADDRESS

USERNAME

PASSWORD

PASSWORD HINTS

APPLICATION/WEB ADDRESS

USERNAME

PASSWORD

PASSWORD HINTS

APPLICATION/WEB ADDRESS

USERNAME

PASSWORD

PASSWORD HINTS

Z

APPLICATION/WEB ADDRESS

USERNAME

PASSWORD

PASSWORD HINTS

APPLICATION/WEB ADDRESS

USERNAME

PASSWORD

PASSWORD HINTS